The Light and the Land

Ireland Yearbook 2002

Paintings from the Ulster Museum

First published by Appletree Press Ltd, 14 Howard Street South, Belfast BT7 1AP
Copyright © Appletree Press 2001. Text © Appletree Press 2001.
Photographs reproduced with the kind permission of the Trustees of the National
Museums and Galleries of Northern Ireland.

Front cover: *Nightfall, Connemara* by Maurice MacGonigal
Back cover: *Blue Shore* by Terence (T. P.) Flanagan

The Light and the Land

Ireland Yearbook 2002

Paintings from the Ulster Museum

Foreword

The Ulster Museum's Fine Art Collections – paintings, sculpture, drawings, watercolours and prints – cover a wide spectrum of works, from the 16th century to the present day.

The Friends of the National Collections of Ireland and the Contemporary Art Society have for many years made generous gifts to the Museum. The help of such grant-awarding bodies as The National Arts Collections Fund, National Heritage Memorial Fund, the Heritage Lottery Fund and the Esmé Mitchell Trust has been instrumental in enabling the Museum to further enhance its Applied Art holdings. These include significant collections of historic Irish glass and silver, alongside furniture, costume, textiles and jewellery.

The museum's historical collection of British and Irish watercolours includes extensive holdings by the 19th-century Belfast artists Andrew Nicholl (1804–86) and Dr James Moore (1819–83).

With collections spanning Irish, British, continental European and North American items, the Museum has the most comprehensive assembly of 20th-century art in Ireland.

The Ulster Museum is part of the National Museums and Galleries of Northern Ireland.

Farm and Trees
1960

Kenneth Webb (born London 1927)

Oil on board 33.5 x 89cm

The Irish landscape has inspired Kenneth Webb throughout his career: in 1957, after having been head of the painting school at Belfast College of Art, he founded the Irish School of Landscape Painting, and since the 1970s he has painted around his studio cottage in Connemara. Webb, along with Maurice Wilks, is an exponent of a free, expresionistic landscape genre and his compositions are generally wide in format. He is also noted for his use of primary colours – here the beautiful cobalt-blues of the sky and horizon, the red of the farm building doors and window and lush green patches of grass add richness to a wintry scene of spiky trees, eerily lacking human presence. The painting was given to the Ulster Museum by the Thomas Haverty Trust in 1996, which bought it from the Ritchie Hendricks Gallery in Dublin.

December 2001

M		3	10	17	24	31
T		4	11	18	25
W		5	12	19	26
T		6	13	20	27
F		7	14	21	28
S	1	8	15	22	29
S	2	9	16	23	30

January 2002

M		7	14	21	28
T	1	8	15	22	29
W	2	9	16	23	30
T	3	10	17	24	31
F	4	11	18	25
S	5	12	19	26
S	6	13	20	27

February 2002

M		4	11	18	25
T		5	12	19	26
W		6	13	20	27
T		7	14	21	28
F	1	8	15	22
S	2	9	16	23
S	3	10	17	24

DECEMBER 2001

MONDAY 24

THURSDAY 27

TUESDAY 25

FRIDAY 28

WEDNESDAY 26

SATURDAY 29 / SUNDAY 30

DECEMBER 2001 / JANUARY 2002

MONDAY 31

THURSDAY 3

TUESDAY 1

FRIDAY 4

WEDNESDAY 2

SATURDAY 5 / SUNDAY 6

Tory in a Storm
c.1977

Patsy Dan Rodgers (born Tory Island, active since 1960s)
Acrylic on board 79.2 x 67.7cm

Patsy Dan Rodgers (Patsy Dan Mac Ruaidhri) is the honorary "King" of Tory Island, the isolated and treeless island off Horn Head, Co. Donegal that is home to about 170 Gaelic-speaking residents. Rodgers is a second generation artist from a Tory Island School of painters (*see also James Dixon's* Mr William Rogers Plowing, *Week 34*), whose work is characterised by a primitive, often perspectiveless style, using bold colours and sometimes humour. In this naïve aerial view, Rodgers conveys the charm of the island's key buildings, including the lighthouse complex, set amidst the emptiness of surrounding fields. The waves splashing against the rocks and cliffs all around the island add dynamism to the seascape and emphasise the contours of the isolated landscape. The Ulster Museum purchased the painting in 1977 after it was exhibited in Belfast.

TORY

P.D.Rodgers.

JANUARY 2002

MONDAY 7

THURSDAY 10

TUESDAY 8

FRIDAY 11

WEDNESDAY 9

SATURDAY 12 / SUNDAY 13

JANUARY 2002

MONDAY 14

THURSDAY 17

TUESDAY 15

FRIDAY 18

WEDNESDAY 16

SATURDAY 19 / SUNDAY 20

Nightfall, Connemara
c.1962

Maurice MacGonigal (born Dublin 1900; died Dublin 1979)
Oil on board 50.7 x 75.9cm

Maurice MacGonigal started out as a stained glass artist. He trained in the studio of his uncle, Joshua Clarke, where his cousin, the notable stained glass artist Harry Clarke, also worked. MacGonigal turned to painting and went on to become President of the Royal Hibernian Academy; he was also father of the art critic Ciaran MacGonigal. He stated that this painting was executed on the spot, a short distance from Roundstone, Connemara, close to the junction of the "bog road" to Clifden and the road from Roundstone to Cashel. It was late evening, in the afterlight. The painting was shown in the Oireachtas Exhibition in Dublin in 1962 and bought by the Thomas Haverty Trust, which presented it to the Ulster Museum.

December 2001

M		3	10	17	24	31
T		4	11	18	25	
W		5	12	19	26	
T		6	13	20	27	
F		7	14	21	28	
S	1	8	15	22	29	
S	2	9	16	23	30	

January 2002

M		7	14	21	28	
T	1	8	15	22	29	
W	2	9	16	23	30	
T	3	10	17	24	31	
F	4	11	18	25		
S	5	12	19	26		
S	6	13	20	27		

February 2002

M		4	11	18	25
T		5	12	19	26
W		6	13	20	27
T		7	14	21	28
F	1	8	15	22	
S	2	9	16	23	
S	3	10	17	24	

JANUARY 2002

MONDAY 21

THURSDAY 24

TUESDAY 22

FRIDAY 25

WEDNESADY 23

SATURDAY 26 / SUNDAY 27

JANUARY/FEBRUARY 2002

MONDAY 28

THURSDAY 31

TUESDAY 29

FRIDAY 1

WEDNESDAY 30

SATURDAY 2 / SUNDAY 3

Ruin at Ardmore, Co. Waterford

c.1946

Evie Hone (born Roebuck Grove, Dublin 1894; died Rathfarnham, Dublin 1955)
Oil on panel 46.3 x 55.2cm

Evie Hone's family line included the artists Nathaniel Hone the Elder (1718–84) and Younger (1831–1917). While partially disabled by infant paralysis which required much treatment and necessitated visits to England, France and Italy, she was set on being an artist. A visit to Assisi in 1911 made a deep religious impression on her, and her spirituality developed profoundly throughout her life. She studied under Sickert and Meninsky in London, and in 1920 she and Mainie Jellett (*see Week 48*) went to Paris to become pupils of André Lhôte, and later of the cubist painter Albert Gleizes. Hone and Jellett became pioneers of 'modern' painting in Ireland, although in the later 1920s Hone's work became brighter, more figurative and less abstract. She converted from Anglicanism to Catholicism in 1937 and began painting stained glass (notably designing the East Window for Eton College Chapel). She opened a studio in Rathfarnham in 1943. Ardmore's monastic ruins held a special fascination for Hone, her enthusiasm for the place evidenced in this oil by the strong colours of the sky, hills and churchyard, and in the dynamic, rhythmic diagonal lines of the composition.

FEBRUARY 2002

MONDAY 4

THURSDAY 7

TUESDAY 5

FRIDAY 8

WEDNESDAY 6

SATURDAY 9 / SUNDAY 10

FEBRUARY 2002

MONDAY 11

THURSDAY 14

TUESDAY 12

FRIDAY 15

WEDNESDAY 13

SATURDAY 16 / SUNDAY 17

Bog Reflection

1960–61

Patrick Scott (born Cork 1921)

Tempera on canvas on board 61 x 50.8cm

Although always more interested in art, Scott trained as an architect at University College Dublin. He remained in that profession as a partner of Michael Scott and Associates until 1960, when he decided to paint full time. He was a member of the White Stag Group and exhibited at the White Stag Gallery as early as 1941; he was also a member of the Irish Living Art Group. Scott worked as a designer too, producing, amongst other things, corporate identity and colour schemes for CIE and a series of carpets for Kilkenny Design Workshops. An honorary member of the Royal Hibernian Academy, he is still active as a painter – his work is displayed widely and in many private collections. He has been described as upholding "the values of a quiet, tasteful, contemplative form of abstraction", in notable contrast to Action Painting which was popular during much of his career. The artist's contemplative approach is evident in this subtle, abstract work and even, perhaps, in the double-meaning of the title.

January 2002

M		7	14	21	28
T	1	8	15	22	29
W	2	9	16	23	30
T	3	10	17	24	31
F	4	11	18	25	
S	5	12	19	26	
S	6	13	20	27	

February 2002

M		4	11	18	25
T		5	12	19	26
W		6	13	20	27
T		7	14	21	28
F	1	8	15	22	
S	2	9	16	23	
S	3	10	17	24	

March 2002

M		4	11	18	25
T		5	12	19	26
W		6	13	20	27
T		7	14	21	28
F	1	8	15	22	29
S	2	9	16	23	30
S	3	10	17	24	31

FEBRUARY 2002

MONDAY 18

THURSDAY 21

TUESDAY 19

FRIDAY 22

WEDNESDAY 20

SATURDAY 23 / SUNDAY 24

F E B R U A R Y / M A R C H   2 0 0 2

MONDAY 25

THURSDAY 28

TUESDAY 26

FRIDAY 1

WEDNESDAY 27

SATURDAY 2 / SUNDAY 3

Ringsend from Beggar's Bush, Co. Dublin

Francis Danby (born nr. Killinick, Wexford 1793; died Exmouth 1861)
Watercolour on paper 20.8 x 30.5cm

Left penniless after the death of his father, Francis Danby studied for a short time at the Dublin Society Drawing Schools, where he became friendly with the landscape painters, James Arthur O'Connor and George Petrie (*see Week 36*). Together they went to the Royal Academy exhibition in London in 1813, after which Danby settled in Bristol, though he led a precarious existence there. In 1824 he moved to London where his paintings were widely admired, but in 1829 he was defeated in election to full membership of the Royal Academy by one vote – by John Constable. This gentle watercolour with its big, rather watery sky is one of just a few early Irish paintings. The scene of Ringsend from Beggar's Bush – both of which are now suburbs of Dublin, south of where the River Liffey enters Dublin Bay – shows evidence of man's visual impact on the landscape: tall ships masts and a large smoking chimney the backdrop to open shoreline grassland.

February 2002

M		4	11	18	25
T		5	12	19	26
W		6	13	20	27
T		7	14	21	28
F	1	8	15	22	
S	2	9	16	23	
S	3	10	17	24	

March 2002

M		4	11	18	25
T		5	12	19	26
W		6	13	20	27
T		7	14	21	28
F	1	8	15	22	29
S	2	9	16	23	30
S	3	10	17	24	31

April 2001

M	1	8	15	22	29
T	2	9	16	23	30
W	3	10	17	24	
T	4	11	18	25	
F	5	12	19	26	
S	6	13	20	27	
S	7	14	21	28	

MARCH 2002

MONDAY 4

THURSDAY 7

TUESDAY 5

FRIDAY 8

WEDNESDAY 6

SATURDAY 9 / SUNDAY 10

MARCH 2002

MONDAY 11

THURSDAY 14

TUESDAY 12

FRIDAY 15

WEDNESDAY 13

SATURDAY 16 / SUNDAY 17

A Road

Basil Blackshaw (born Glengormley, Co. Antrim 1923)
Charcoal, white on paper 38.5 x 56cm

Brought up in Boardmills, Co. Down, Basil Blackshaw attended Methodist College, Belfast and later studied at the Belfast College of Art along with T.P. Flanagan. The poet John Hewitt, onetime Keeper of Art in the Ulster Museum, quickly became one of his early patrons. Blackshaw's work explores variations on recurring themes – horses, dogs and animal trainers and breeders form part of his subject-matter – but an interest in the landscape and people closely associated with the land is frequently evident. His style is reductionist – paring down to the essentials. This sketch, with its strong, scratchy lines like etching, forms an evocative depiction of isolation; the telegraph poles leading along the empty road to the lonely dwellings is the only sign of life existing beside a flat sea. The Ulster Museum purchased the work in 1963.

February 2002

M		4	11	18	25
T		5	12	19	26
W		6	13	20	27
T		7	14	21	28
F	1	8	15	22	
S	2	9	16	23	
S	3	10	17	24	

March 2002

M		4	11	18	25
T		5	12	19	26
W		6	13	20	27
T		7	14	21	28
F	1	8	15	22	29
S	2	9	16	23	30
S	3	10	17	24	31

April 2001

M	1	8	15	22	29
T	2	9	16	23	30
W	3	10	17	24	
T	4	11	18	25	
F	5	12	19	26	
S	6	13	20	27	
S	7	14	21	28	

MARCH 2002

MONDAY 18

THURSDAY 21

TUESDAY 19

FRIDAY 22

WEDNESDAY 20

SATURDAY 23 / SUNDAY 24

Week 13

MONDAY 25

THURSDAY 28

TUESDAY 26

FRIDAY 29

WEDNESDAY 27

SATURDAY 30 / SUNDAY 31

Peat Stacks

Arthur Gilmer (born 1882; died 1929)
Pencil, chalk on paper 15.9 x 24cm

Very little is actually known about Arthur Gilmer. In the Belfast Directory of 1909, "Alfred" Gilmer, painter, is noted as living at 46 Damascus Street. But, in 1914, Arthur Gilmer exhibited two pictures at the Royal Hibernian Academy, giving an address of 35 Wellington Place, Belfast. "A Gilmer" was still recorded at that address in the Belfast Directory of 1921–2, which lists it as the headquarters of the Irish Decorative Art Association. This sketch – one of a group – shows Gilmer to have been a sensitive observer of the landscape (he also painted the Dublin townscape), in a style reminiscent of Paul Henry. The scene depicting the mound of peat is rendered in subtle tones; compositionally, the ditch provides a central visual lead. The scene is very similar to his *Cruaghgorm From Pollagh Bog* (1927) which locates the landscape as the rolling hills of the Blue Stack Mountains in south Donegal (below here Lough Eske drains into Eske River which flows into Atlantic through Donegal Town).

March 2002

M		4	11	18	25
T		5	12	19	26
W		6	13	20	27
T		7	14	21	28
F	1	8	15	22	29
S	2	9	16	23	30
S	3	10	17	24	31

April 2001

M	1	8	15	22	29
T	2	9	16	23	30
W	3	10	17	24	
T	4	11	18	25	
F	5	12	19	26	
S	6	13	20	27	
S	7	14	21	28	

May 2001

M		6	13	20	27
T		7	14	21	28
W	1	8	15	22	29
T	2	9	16	23	30
F	4	10	17	24	31
S	5	11	18	25	
S	5	12	19	26	

APRIL 2002

MONDAY 1

THURSDAY 4

TUESDAY 2

FRIDAY 5

WEDNESDAY 3

SATURDAY 6 / SUNDAY 7

MONDAY 8

THURSDAY 11

TUESDAY 9

FRIDAY 12

WEDNESDAY 10

SATURDAY 13 / SUNDAY 14

Breakers, Achill
1953

Patric Stevenson (born Wadhurst, Sussex 1909; died Hillsborough, Co. Down 1983)
Gouache on paper 30.1 x 44.4cm

The son of a former Rector of Rathlin and Dean of Waterford, Patric Stevenson was educated at Methodist College, Belfast, the Belfast School of Art (1926–8) and the Slade School in London. After some time living in England, he returned to Ireland in 1950 and was elected to the Royal Ulster Academy in 1959, eventually becoming its President from 1970 to 1976. He pioneered open-air exhibitions in the 1950s and 60s, first in Rostrevor and then at the Shambles in Hillsborough, Co. Down. This painting is bold and brooding with its strong foreground of age-old rocks and boulders. The rolling breakers reveal a greeny-blue sea with disquieting patches of black suggesting the darker depths beneath the surface. The oppressive greyness of the wet sky is only slightly relieved by the presence of a gentle grassy headland. The artist would seem to possess an islander's preoccupation of staring out to sea and a fascination of watching the seascape and weather constantly change.

APRIL 2002

MONDAY 15

THURSDAY 18

TUESDAY 16

FRIDAY 19

WEDNESDAY 17

SATURDAY 20 / SUNDAY 21

MONDAY 22

THURSDAY 25

TUESDAY 23

FRIDAY 26

WEDNESDAY 24

SATURDAY 27 / SUNDAY 28

Village by the Sea
1953

Norah Allison McGuinness (born Derry 1903; died Dublin 1980)
Oil on canvas 68.9 x 91.6cm

Norah McGuinness, the daughter of a Derry merchant, attended classes at the Derry Technical School before entering the Metropolitan School of Art, Dublin, in 1921. She studied under the painter Patrick Tuohy, the designer Oswald Reeves and the stained glass artist Harry Clarke, and went on to design costumes and sets for the Abbey and Peacock Theatres. On the advice of Mainie Jellett (*see Week 48*), and after the break up of her marriage to Geoffrey Taylor in 1929, she went to Paris to study under André Lhôte, but she did not care for his academic cubism; rather she was influenced by Raoul Dufy and Georges Braque, amongst others. After travels in Europe and India and periods of living in London and America, she returned to Dublin in 1939 where she worked as a window designer for Brown Thomas's department store and also resumed her stage design. In 1944, she succeeded Mainie Jellett as President of the Irish Exhibition of Living Art; her painting was spontaneous and unacademic, often showing a Fauvist influence. *Village by the Sea* was painted in 1953 in Dunmore East, Co. Waterford, and was lent by the artist to the Irish Exhibition of Living Art that year.

March 2002

M		4	11	18	25
T		5	12	19	26
W		6	13	20	27
T		7	14	21	28
F	1	8	15	22	29
S	2	9	16	23	30
S	3	10	17	24	31

April 2002

M	1	8	15	22	29
T	2	9	16	23	30
W	3	10	17	24	
T	4	11	18	25	
F	5	12	19	26	
S	6	13	20	27	
S	7	14	21	28	

May 2002

M		6	13	20	27
T		7	14	21	28
W	1	8	15	22	29
T	2	9	16	23	30
F	4	10	17	24	31
S	5	11	18	25	
S	5	12	19	26	

APRIL/MAY 2002

MONDAY 29

THURSDAY 2

TUESDAY 30

FRIDAY 3

WEDNESDAY 1

SATURDAY 4 / SUNDAY 5

MAY 2002

MONDAY 6

THURSDAY 9

TUESDAY 7

FRIDAY 10

WEDNESDAY 8

SATURDAY 11 / SUNDAY 12

Red Mill, Whitehouse
1948

Arthur M. Campbell (Born Belfast 1909; died Belfast 1994)
Pencil, watercolour on card 38.4 x 50.5cm

Arthur Campbell, son of Gretta Bowen and brother of George Campbell, was part of the notable group of Northern artists known as the "Irish Figurists" which included his brother George, Gerard Dillon, Gladys Maccabe, Daniel O'Neill and Markey Robinson. Arthur, however, preferred landscape over figurative painting; he was also a passionate photographer, and won the Royal Dublin Society's Art Award in 1936. The Council for the Encouragement of Music and the Arts (CEMA) mounted a one-man show in 1950, but between the 1950s and 1970s he ceased to exhibit due to a busy career in publicity for the car industry. The industrial landscape of Belfast's Red Mill obviously fascinated him – a crayon sketch dated 1958 also exists. The single foreground figure walking amongst the dark shacks appears isolated against the brooding presence of the mill – the first cotton mill in Ireland, founded by Nicholas Grimshaw in 1784, it employed 1,000 people and was the cradle of Ireland's industrial revolution.

April 2002

M	1	8	15	22	29
T	2	9	16	23	30
W	3	10	17	24	
T	4	11	18	25	
F	5	12	19	26	
S	6	13	20	27	
S	7	14	21	28	

May 2002

M		6	13	20	27	
T		7	14	21	28	
W	1	8	15	22	29	
T	2	9	16	23	30	
F	4	10	17	24	31	
S	5	11	18	25		
S	5	12	19	26		

June 2002

M		3	10	17	24
T		4	11	18	25
W		5	12	19	26
T		6	13	20	27
F		7	14	21	28
S	1	8	15	22	29
S	2	9	16	23	30

Arthur M. Campbell

MAY 2002

MONDAY 13

THURSDAY 16

TUESDAY 14

FRIDAY 17

WEDNESDAY 15

SATURDAY 18 / SUNDAY 19

MAY 2002

MONDAY 20

THURSDAY 23

TUESDAY 21

FRIDAY 24

WEDNESDAY 22

SATURDAY 25 / SUNDAY 26

Summer Evening, Achill

Michael J. de Burca (born Dublin 1914; died Dublin 1985)
Armagh County Museum
Oil on board 45.5 x 50.5cm

Born Michael J. Bourke, de Burca Gaelicised his name and exhibited regularly at the Royal Hibernian Academy between 1933 and 1976, giving most of his paintings Gaelic titles. From 1938 to 1969 he was on the staff of the National College of Art in Dublin, but moved to Westport, Co. Mayo in the 1970s. This pleasing depiction of the coastline near Westport goes beyond depicting the landscape with its peat bog and ditch and seascape glistening in the summer sunshine, by including both animal and human elements, with the man and woman perhaps in dialogue. de Burca's work was favoured by the Thomas Haverty Trust, which presented this particular painting to Armagh Museum, along with a large caricatural watercolour to the Ulster Museum.

April 2002

M	1	8	15	22	29
T	2	9	16	23	30
W	3	10	17	24	
T	4	11	18	25	
F	5	12	19	26	
S	6	13	20	27	
S	7	14	21	28	

May 2002

M		6	13	20	27
T		7	14	21	28
W	1	8	15	22	29
T	2	9	16	23	30
F	4	10	17	24	31
S	5	11	18	25	
S	5	12	19	26	

June 2002

M		3	10	17	24
T		4	11	18	25
W		5	12	19	26
T		6	13	20	27
F		7	14	21	28
S	1	8	15	22	29
S	2	9	16	23	30

MAY/JUNE 2002

MONDAY 27

THURSDAY 30

TUESDAY 28

FRIDAY 31

WEDNESDAY 29

SATURDAY 1 / SUNDAY 2

JUNE 2002

MONDAY 3

THURSDAY 6

TUESDAY 4

FRIDAY 7

WEDNESDAY 5

SATURDAY 8 / SUNDAY 9

City of Armagh

1810

James Black (died Armagh 1829)
Armagh County Museum
Oil on canvas 92.2 x 132.3cm

This bright and colourful view of Armagh is a good example of the city landscape in the early nineteenth century. It was sold by raffle to a tanner called Robert Steen, and later passed into the hands of a Mr Dobbin before being presented to the Town Commissioners. In the centre of the painting is the Church of Ireland Cathedral of St Patrick on its hill, replete with a spire which was later removed by Archbishop Beresford. On the left, the Windmill with its sails is visible, as is the three-gabled wall of St Malachy's Chapel built in 1752 (later demolished). The Market Cross is visible *in situ* – it was later removed to the cathedral during rioting in 1813. Also recognisable is Abbey Street Presbyterian Church of 1722 on the right; the Courthouse erected in 1809; the Mall surrounded by trees; the buildings of the Royal School; and the back of the Gaol on the extreme right. The artist, a Scottish protestant better known as a portrait painter, came to an unfortunate end, although the details surrounding his death are a matter of dispute. Either interfering in some domestic argument or involved in a sectarian altercation near his home in Lower English Street, he was struck on the head with a cleaver by a butcher called Thomas Feely when returning home from an Orange Lodge meeting. Black died two days later, and Feely absconded, after having removed his victim from his own house to the artist's lodgings the morning after the incident.

JUNE 2002

MONDAY 10

THURSDAY 13

TUESDAY 11

FRIDAY 14

WEDNESDAY 12

SATURDAY 15 / SUNDAY 16

JUNE 2002

MONDAY 17

THURSDAY 20

TUESDAY 18

FRIDAY 21

WEDNESDAY 19

SATURDAY 22/ SUNDAY 23

Surge of the Sea, Ardglass

Hans Iten (born Zürich 1874; died Bulach, Switzerland 1930)
Oil on board 26.9 x 34.8cm

Hans Iten, though Swiss, spent most of his working life in Belfast as a damask designer with the linen firm of McCrum, Watson and Mercer in Linenhall Street. One of the most accomplished painters in the city at the time, Iten was an active member of the Belfast Art Society. He exhibited widely – at the Paris Salon, the Glasgow Institute, the Royal Academy and the Royal Hibernian Academy. Iten maintained his continental links throughout his life, and died in Switzerland while convalescing after an operation. The Ulster Museum holds several of the artist's works, as well as portraits of him by George Kane and Pierre Montézin. Iten painted Ardglass in Co. Down *en plein air* many times (the Museum also holds another Ardglass scene, *Her Little Holding*, for example) and it was one of his favourite localities, where he knew many people. *Surge of the Sea* is colourful and playful (the seagulls are expressed as simple light brushstrokes), and the thick impasto and strong hues hint at a Fauvist-like expressionism.

May 2002

M		6	13	20	27
T		7	14	21	28
W	1	8	15	22	29
T	2	9	16	23	30
F	4	10	17	24	31
S	5	11	18	25	
S	5	12	19	26	

June 2002

M		3	10	17	24
T		4	11	18	25
W		5	12	19	26
T		6	13	20	27
F		7	14	21	28
S	1	8	15	22	29
S	2	9	16	23	30

July 2002

M	1	8	15	22	29
T	2	9	16	23	30
W	3	10	17	24	31
T	4	11	18	25	
F	5	12	19	26	
S	6	13	20	27	
S	7	14	21	28	

JUNE 2002

MONDAY 24

THURSDAY 27

TUESDAY 25

FRIDAY 28

WEDNESDAY 26

SATURDAY 29 / SUNDAY 30

JULY 2002

MONDAY 1

THURSDAY 4

TUESDAY 2

FRIDAY 5

WEDNESDAY 3

SATURDAY 6 / SUNDAY 7

Haystacks
1933

Annie Florence Violet McAdoo (born Cookstown, Co. Tyrone 1896; died Belfast 1961)
Watercolour on paper 22.5 x 29.7cm

Violet McAdoo trained at the Belfast School of Art and at the Royal College of Art – where she took her Associateship in 1927 – and was an accomplished and confident watercolourist. She was art mistress at Princess Gardens girls' school in Belfast, although had to retire early due to poor health. She was active in and exhibited paintings at the Society of Watercolour Artists, Royal Hibernian Academy and Royal Ulster Academy. This simple but bold depiction of a rural landscape scene from the thirties uses watercolours of subtle golden tones to capture the late summer mood. McAdoo seems interested in the strong visual presence that the haystacks create in the field – they are striking and dominant forms, carefully made, almost like houses, but only temporary 'structures' in the landscape. The painting was donated to the Ulster Museum by J.F. Hunter ARCA in 1937.

June 2002

M		3	10	17	24
T		4	11	18	25
W		5	12	19	26
T		6	13	20	27
F		7	14	21	28
S	1	8	15	22	29
S	2	9	16	23	30

July 2002

M	1	8	15	22	29
T	2	9	16	23	30
W	3	10	17	24	31
T	4	11	18	25
F	5	12	19	26
S	6	13	20	27
S	7	14	21	28

August 2002

M		5	12	19	26
T		6	13	20	27
W		7	14	21	28
T	1	8	15	22	29
F	2	9	16	23	30
S	3	10	17	24	31
S	4	11	18	25

V. McAdoo '33

JULY 2002

MONDAY 8

THURSDAY 11

TUESDAY 9

FRIDAY 12

WEDNESDAY 10

SATURDAY 13 / SUNDAY 14

MONDAY 15

THURSDAY 18

TUESDAY 16

FRIDAY 19

WEDNESDAY 17

SATURDAY 20 / SUNDAY 21

The Potato Gatherers

George William Russell ("AE") (born Lurgan 1867; died Bournemouth 1935)
Armagh County Museum
Oil on canvas 50.7 x 61cm

George William Russell, known as "AE", was something of a polymath in Irish life – a painter, poet, writer, economist, philosopher and mystic. He studied art at evening classes in the Royal Hibernian Academy Schools and the Metropolitan School of Art, Dublin, and his landscapes are usually peopled and often ethereal. This painting formerly belonged to Lily Yeats, sister of the poet W.B. Yeats and the painter Jack Butler Yeats. It shows "AE" using a broadly painted objective style reminiscent of the French painter Jean-Claude Millet. The artist's work also shows the influence of the young Paul Henry. Russell was deeply involved in Irish rural affairs as the editor of the agricultural magazine *Irish Homestead* from 1905 to 1923. Armagh County Museum has twenty-two paintings by this, one of the county's most renowned native sons.

June 2002

M		3	10	17	24
T		4	11	18	25
W		5	12	19	26
T		6	13	20	27
F		7	14	21	28
S	1	8	15	22	29
S	2	9	16	23	30

July 2002

M	1	8	15	22	29
T	2	9	16	23	30
W	3	10	17	24	31
T	4	11	18	25	
F	5	12	19	26	
S	6	13	20	27	
S	7	14	21	28	

August 2002

M		5	12	19	26
T		6	13	20	27
W		7	14	21	28
T	1	8	15	22	29
F	2	9	16	23	30
S	3	10	17	24	31
S	4	11	18	25	

JULY 2002

MONDAY 22

THURSDAY 25

TUESDAY 23

FRIDAY 26

WEDNESDAY 24

SATURDAY 27 / SUNDAY 28

JULY/AUGUST 2002

MONDAY 29

THURSDAY 1

TUESDAY 30

FRIDAY 2

WEDNESDAY 31

SATURDAY 3 / SUNDAY 4

Long Walk from Claddagh Quay, Galway
1987

Cecil Maguire (born Lurgan 1930)
Armagh County Museum
Oil on board 61 x 45.5cm

Cecil Maguire was born in Lurgan, Co. Armagh, graduated from Queen's University, Belfast in 1951, and was for many years Senior Master at Lurgan College; he was mainly self-taught as a painter. He was elected to membership of the Royal Ulster Academy in 1974 and his work is represented in many private, corporate and public collections. He now lives in Connemara where he finds inspiration for much of his work. He treats his subject matter – which ranges from animals and fair days in market towns to the West of Ireland landscape – in a highly realistic way, imbuing his paintings with different qualities of light. Boats are also a favourite subject – here tied up on the quay on a quiet but overcast day. The reflections of waterfront buildings and the shadows of the boats and their masts in the slightly murky water make for a calming scene, albeit one with the hint of Galway city's industrial backdrop included.

July 2002

M	1	8	15	22	29
T	2	9	16	23	30
W	3	10	17	24	31
T	4	11	18	25	
F	5	12	19	26	
S	6	13	20	27	
S	7	14	21	28	

August 2002

M		5	12	19	26
T		6	13	20	27
W		7	14	21	28
T	1	8	15	22	29
F	2	9	16	23	30
S	3	10	17	24	31
S	4	11	18	25	

September 2002

M		2	9	16	23	30
T		3	10	17	24	
W		4	11	18	25	
T		5	12	19	26	
F		6	13	20	27	
S		7	14	21	28	
S	1	8	15	22	29	

AUGUST 2002

MONDAY 5

THURSDAY 8

TUESDAY 6

FRIDAY 9

WEDNESDAY 7

SATURDAY 10 / SUNDAY 11

AUGUST 2002

MONDAY 12

THURSDAY 15

TUESDAY 13

FRIDAY 16

WEDNESDAY 14

SATURDAY 17 / SUNDAY 18

Mr William Rogers Plowing (sic) in Dixon Farm Tory Island: The First Tractor That Ever Came to Tory Island
1967

James Dixon (born Tory Island 1887; died Tory Island 1970)
Oil on paper on board 57.2 x 76cm

The artist Derek Hill came to Tory Island, off the north coast of Donegal, to paint in the 1960s; watching him work outdoors, local farmer James Dixon told him he could do better. Hill encouraged Dixon, giving him paints and paper and offering him brushes, but he preferred to fashion his own with hair from his donkey's tail. Dixon went on to become the "father" of a school of primitive painters on Tory Island and his house in An Baile Thair has been converted into an art gallery. His brother John, Patsy Dan Rodgers (*see Week 2*), Ruari Rodgers, Michael Finbar Rodgers and Anton Meenan followed Dixon's example. One of Dixon's techniques was to scrape into the wet paint with the end of his brush handle – deployed here to indicate the lines of the ploughed field. The Tory painters' style was generally perspectiveless – here there is the mixed aerial viewpoint of the field with birds hovering above and bright specks of flowers, combined with a side-on view of the notable tractor and livestock in the field to left of the ploughed tract.

July 2002

M	1	8	15	22	29
T	2	9	16	23	30
W	3	10	17	24	31
T	4	11	18	25	
F	5	12	19	26	
S	6	13	20	27	
S	7	14	21	28	

August 2002

M		5	12	19	26
T		6	13	20	27
W		7	14	21	28
T	1	8	15	22	29
F	2	9	16	23	30
S	3	10	17	24	31
S	4	11	18	25	

September 2002

M		2	9	16	23	30
T		3	10	17	24	
W		4	11	18	25	
T		5	12	19	26	
F		6	13	20	27	
S		7	14	21	28	
S	1	8	15	22	29	

AUGUST 2002

MONDAY 19

THURSDAY 22

TUESDAY 20

FRIDAY 23

WEDNESDAY 21

SATURDAY 24 / SUNDAY 25

AUGUST/SEPTEMBER 2002

MONDAY 26

THURSDAY 29

TUESDAY 27

FRIDAY 30

WEDNESDAY 28

SATURDAY 31 / SUNDAY 1

Holy Island, Lough Derg, Co. Clare

c. 1863

Bartholomew Colles Watkins (born Dublin 1833 died Dublin 1891)

Oil on canvas 104.3 x 153cm

The full title of the work is *Ecclesiastical Ruins on Inniscaltra, or Holy Island, Lough Derg, Co. Clare, after* Sunset: "This Island is One of Great Historic Interest…" – *Petrie (c.1863)*. The artist of the painting on which this one is based was the landscape painter George Petrie, a contemporary of Francis Danby and James Arthur O'Connor at the Dublin Drawing Schools (*see Week 10*). Bartholomew Colles Watkins devoted himself to painting Irish landscapes in a particularly detailed style and was a regular exhibitor at the Royal Hibernian Academy from 1860 onwards. He was particularly fond of painting scenes around Connemara and Killarney. He worked slowly and meticulously and as a result his output was relatively small. This is a very good example of his work showing the monastic ruins of an ancient place of Irish pilgrimage against an evocative sunset. The monastery was founded in the 7th century by St Caimin and the ruins are, left to right, St Mary's Church, St Brigid's Church, the Round Tower, St Caimin's Church and an anchorite's cell.

SEPTEMBER 2002

MONDAY 2

THURSDAY 5

TUESDAY 3

FRIDAY 6

WEDNESDAY 4

SATURDAY 7 / FRIDAY 8

SEPTEMBER 2002

MONDAY 9

THURSDAY 12

TUESDAY 10

FRIDAY 13

WEDNESDAY 11

SATURDAY 14 /SUNDAY 15

September Evening, Ballymote
1951

Colin Middleton (born Belfast 1910; died Bangor, Co. Down 1983)
Oil on canvas 50.8 x 76.4cm

Colin Middleton was the son of a damask designer who in 1927 went into his father's trade. He studied at the same time at Belfast School of Art under Newton Penprase and in 1935 he was made an Associate of the Royal Ulster Academy; he exhibited for the first time at the Royal Hibernian Academy in 1941. Middleton attributed his feelings for texture and material to his training in the damask business, but he was also impressed by the work of Vincent Van Gogh, whose work he saw on a visit to London in 1928. Van Gogh's influence is detectable in the use of warm, rich colours applied with thick brushstroke in this depiction of the undulating Co. Sligo landscape at twilight. Middleton said about landcape: "When you get there, you know you belong … it gets you, it eats you". Many of Middleton's paintings from the 1940s and 1950s are skilfully handled in an "expressionistic" style.

August 2002

M		5	12	19	26
T		6	13	20	27
W		7	14	21	28
T	1	8	15	22	29
F	2	9	16	23	30
S	3	10	17	24	31
S	4	11	18	25	

September 2002

M		2	9	16	23	30
T		3	10	17	24	
W		4	11	18	25	
T		5	12	19	26	
F		6	13	20	27	
S		7	14	21	28	
S	1	8	15	22	29	

October 2002

M		7	14	21	28
T	1	8	15	22	29
W	2	9	16	23	30
T	3	10	17	24	31
F	4	11	18	25	
S	5	12	19	26	
S	6	13	20	27	

SEPTEMBER 2002

MONDAY 16

THURSDAY 19

TUESDAY 17

FRIDAY 20

WEDNESDAY 18

SATURDAY 21 / SUNDAY 22

SEPTEMBER 2002

MONDAY 23

THURSDAY 26

TUESDAY 24

FRIDAY 27

WEDNESDAY 25

SATURDAY 28 / SUNDAY 29

The Lifting of the Fog at the Gasworks, Belfast

c.1926

Georgina Moutray Kyle (born Craigavad, Co. Down 1865; died Belfast 1950)

Oil on canvas 55.1 x 73.5cm

Georgina Moutray Kyle, the daughter of a successful businessman who supplied linens to Queen Victoria, was financially independent enough to give many of her paintings away (and enjoy a somewhat eccentric reputation). She studied at the Academie Colarossi in Paris and went on to exhibit at and become Vice President of the Belfast Art Society; when the society became the Ulster Academy of Arts, she was elected an Academician in 1930. She exhibited regularly at home – enjoying a one-woman Ulster Artists Exhibition in 1945–6 – and at the Paris Salon. This depiction of Belfast's industrialised landscape in the 1920s, executed from a spot on the Ormeau Embankment, is striking. The strong forms of the gasworks set against the backdrop of the hills, painted in dark and gloomy colours, present a dank and brooding fog-bound atmosphere. The church spires and chimneys indicate Belfast's burgeoning cityscape. Low buildings near the massive gas towers appear to "drip" from their roofs down into the murky banks of the River Lagan where the reflections are strongly echoed and distorted – Kyle has captured an oozy translucent quality to the water. The artist seems particularly interested in the formal qualities of the swirling patterns in the water, possibly hinting at a Japanese influence on her style.

SEPTEMBER / OCTOBER 2002

MONDAY 30

THURSDAY 3

TUESDAY 1

FRIDAY 4

WEDNESDAY 2

SATURDAY 5 / SUNDAY 6

OCTOBER 2002

MONDAY 7

THURSDAY 10

TUESDAY 8

FRIDAY 11

WEDNESDAY 9

SATURDAY 12 / SUNDAY 13

Blue Shore

Terence (T.P.) Flanagan (born Enniskillen 1929)
Acrylic on board 63.4 x 76.4cm

Terence – always known as "T.P." – Flanagan attended evening classes at the Technical College in Enniskillen while he was at school and received lessons from Kathleen Bridle, who also taught William Scott. He went on to study at Belfast College of Art, 1949–53, then taught in Lisburn and Ballynahinch, and later at the Belfast College of Art. From 1955 he lectured in art at St Mary's College of Education, Belfast, and was head of the art department there until his retirement in 1984. He works mostly on landscapes, particularly in Donegal and his native Fermanagh. While his work can look very abstract, it almost invariably contains landscape elements. In this painting the elements of the shoreline are merely hinted at: a patch of white indicating water on the sand in the middle ground, and in the foreground an area of colour possibly indicating sand dunes but maybe even a boat. Flanagan often uses oil paint very thinly, as here, in the same way that he uses watercolour.

September 2002

M		2	9	16	23	30
T		3	10	17	24	
W		4	11	18	25	
T		5	12	19	26	
F		6	13	20	27	
S		7	14	21	28	
S	1	8	15	22	29	

October 2002

M		7	14	21	28
T	1	8	15	22	29
W	2	9	16	23	30
T	3	10	17	24	31
F	4	11	18	25	
S	5	12	19	26	
S	6	13	20	27	

November 2002

M		4	11	18	25
T		5	12	19	26
W		6	13	20	27
T		7	14	21	28
F	1	8	15	22	29
S	2	9	16	23	30
S	3	10	17	24	

OCTOBER 2002

MONDAY 14

THURSDAY 17

TUESDAY 15

FRIDAY 18

WEDNESDAY 16

SATURDAY 19 / SUNDAY 20

OCTOBER 2002

MONDAY 21

THURSDAY 24

TUESDAY 22

FRIDAY 25

WEDNESDAY 23

SATURDAY 26 / SUNDAY 27

Glenariff
1935

Henry Echlin Neill (born Belfast 1888; died Belfast 1981)
Pencil, watercolour over pencil on paper 28.8 x 39.5cm

The son of a telegraph overseer, Echlin Neill attended the Belfast School of Art and worked as a lithographic poster artist, employed – like William Conor – by David Allen & Co on Corporation Street, Belfast. Neill later became a draughtsman for the Belfast Corporation Electricity Department. He became a member of the Belfast Art Society in 1912 and went on to be a senior Academician of the Royal Ulster Academy, the Society's successor; he also exhibited at the Royal Hibernian Academy in Dublin. This watercolour of the Glens of Antrim is a typical example of a small, swiftly executed and commercially marketable painting. The landscape of mountains, valleys and glens around Glenariff (or Waterfoot) in Co. Antrim is noted for its lushness and fertility. Here the Glendun River runs down from the Trostan and Sleivenanee peaks into Red Bay beneath. Neill captures the sense of enfolding nature in the Glens in a simple depiction of a homestead embedded in the deep valley, surrounded by luxuriant trees.

OCTOBER/NOVEMBER 2002

MONDAY 28

THURSDAY 31

TUESDAY 29

FRIDAY 1

WEDNESDAY 30

SATURDAY 2 / SUNDAY 3

NOVEMBER 2002

MONDAY 4

THURSDAY 7

TUESDAY 5

FRIDAY 8

WEDNESDAY 6

SATURDAY 9 / SUNDAY 10

Cashel Bay

Ena Douglas (born 1930; died 1963)
Armagh County Museum
Oil on board 30.2 x 40.5cm

Rather little is known about this Irish artist, other than her birth and death dates, that she was the daughter of J.J. Douglas, and married Mr N. Pickard of Dublin. It is also known that Miss Douglas studied at the Metropoint School of Art in Dublin and then at the small independent Byam Shaw School of Art in north London. The painting was purchased for the Armagh County Museum in 1976 at Richhill. The gentle coastal scene with the familiar cottage in the remote landscape shows the artist deploying free handling of the oil paint and using a loose brushstroke, so that the effect is both slightly naïve and yet modern, as well as fresh and charming.

October 2002

M		7	14	21	28
T	1	8	15	22	29
W	2	9	16	23	30
T	3	10	17	24	31
F	4	11	18	25	
S	5	12	19	26	
S	6	13	20	27	

November 2002

M		4	11	18	25
T		5	12	19	26
W		6	13	20	27
T		7	14	21	28
F	1	8	15	22	29
S	2	9	16	23	30
S	3	10	17	24	

December 2002

M		2	9	16	23	30
T		3	10	17	24	31
W		4	11	18	25	
T		5	12	19	26	
F		6	13	20	27	
S		7	14	21	28	
S	1	8	15	22	29	

NOVEMBER 2002

MONDAY 11

THURSDAY 14

TUESDAY 12

FRIDAY 15

WEDNESDAY 13

SATURDAY 16 / SUNDAY 17

NOVEMBER 2002

MONDAY 18

THURSDAY 21

TUESDAY 19

FRIDAY 22

WEDNESDAY 20

SATURDAY 23 / SUNDAY 24

Coast Scene (Dooagh, Achill Island)
1935

Mainie Jellett (born Dublin 1897; died Dublin 1944)
Gouache on paper 25.2 x 35.3cm

October 2002

M		7	14	21	28
T	1	8	15	22	29
W	2	9	16	23	30
T	3	10	17	24	31
F	4	11	18	25
S	5	12	19	26
S	6	13	20	27

November 2002

M		4	11	18	25
T		5	12	19	26
W		6	13	20	27
T		7	14	21	28
F	1	8	15	22	29
S	2	9	16	23	30
S	3	10	17	24

December 2002

M		2	9	16	23	30
T		3	10	17	24	31
W		4	11	18	25
T		5	12	19	26
F		6	13	20	27
S		7	14	21	28
S	1	8	15	22	29

Mainie Jellett, the daughter of a Dublin barrister and a musician, studied at the Metropolitan School of Art under William Orpen and later went to London to study under Walter Sickert at the Westminster School. She was a close friend of Evie Hone (*see Week 6*) and they both went to Paris to André Lhôte's studio and then on to Albert Gleizes' where she developed a Cubist and non-representational style. Back in Ireland, Jellett was a prominent figure in the development of twentieth-century Irish art, through her paintings, lecturing and broadcasting. She did not always work in an abstract way, sometimes returning to semi-abstraction and realism – as in this gouache study of peat cuttings near the coast in the West of Ireland. Often she would make pencil drawings and work them into gouache studies for larger oil paintings later. She also designed carpets and textiles, and sets and costumes for the Gate Theatre; in 1943, the year before her death, she was one of the founders of the Irish Exhibition of Living Art.

NOVEMBER/DECEMBER 2002

MONDAY 25

THURSDAY 28

TUESDAY 26

FRIDAY 29

WEDNESDAY 27

SATURDAY 30 / SUNDAY 1

DECEMBER 2002

MONDAY 2

THURSDAY 5

TUESDAY 3

FRIDAY 6

WEDNESDAY 4

SATURDAY 7 / SUNDAY 8

A Connemara Lake

Charles Lamb (born Portadown 1893; died Carraroe, Connemara 1964)
Oil on board 33.2 x 40.7cm

Charles Lamb was originally apprenticed to his father, a painter and decorator, and in 1913 won a gold medal as the local technical school's best apprentice house painter. He attended evening classes at the Belfast School of Art, and in 1917 won a scholarship to the Metropolitan School of Art, Dublin where he was a pupil of Seán Keating. (He would also have met Paul Henry there, an equally enthusiastic painter of the Connemara landscape.) In 1923 Lamb was elected an associate member of the Royal Hibernian Academy and held his first one-man exhibition. He went to live in a cottage at Carraroe in a remote part of Connemara, and in the 1930s his paintings of the people and landscapes of Connemara were exhibited in Ireland, Britain and the USA. He travelled all over Ireland (in a horse-drawn caravan), started an annual summer school in Carraroe in 1935 and was elected RHA in 1938. His style was contemplative and unintellectual – the gentle blues of this landscape capturing the calm and simplicity of the setting.

November 2002

M		4	11	18	25
T		5	12	19	26
W		6	13	20	27
T		7	14	21	28
F	1	8	15	22	29
S	2	9	16	23	30
S	3	10	17	24	

December 2002

M		2	9	16	23	30
T		3	10	17	24	31
W		4	11	18	25	
T		5	12	19	26	
F		6	13	20	27	
S		7	14	21	28	
S	1	8	15	22	29	

January 2003

M		6	13	20	27	
T		7	14	21	28	
W	1	8	15	22	29	
T	2	9	16	23	30	
F	3	10	17	24	31	
S	4	11	18	25		
S	5	12	19	26		

DECEMBER 2002

MONDAY 9

THURSDAY 12

TUESDAY 10

FRIDAY 13

WEDNESDAY 11

SATURDAY 14 / SUNDAY 15

DECEMBER 2002

MONDAY 16

THURSDAY 19

TUESDAY 17

FRIDAY 20

WEDNESDAY 18

SATURDAY 21 / SUNDAY 22

Newry, Ireland
1812

P.J. or T.[J.P. or T.P.] (19th century)
Ink, wash on paper 18 x 22.9cm

Very little is known about the origins of this small but delightful ink sketch or indeed of its creator – the monogram of the unknown artist is not quite legible but the work is dated September 1812. However, the depiction of the Co. Down town nestling among the mountains is unusual and charming, the more so because the scene looks more Alpine than typically Irish. The view is from a point north-west of Newry looking down over the town and River Bann and across to the Carlingford Mountains.

Newry. Ireland.
Sept. 1812.

DECEMBER 2002

MONDAY 23

THURSDAY 26

TUESDAY 24

FRIDAY 27

WEDNESDAY 25

SATURDAY 28 / SUNDAY 29

DECEMBER/JANUARY 2003

MONDAY 30

THURSDAY 2

TUESDAY 31

FRIDAY 3

WEDNESDAY 1

SATURDAY 4 / SUNDAY 5

Winter Afternoon

1939

Maud Irwin (active Belfast 1912–40)
Watercolour over pencil on card 53.8 x 38cm

Mrs Maud Irwin was a member of the Belfast Art Society (and later the Ulster Academy of Arts), first exhibiting local watercolour views in 1912. There is something of a daydream quality to this large and competent study of a winter scene from what is presumably an upper level window – the viewer and artist look at something and nothing at the same time. The scene over the snow-covered roofs of central Belfast captures a time of day in winter when the sky is heavy and there is no activity at this level above the streets. The artist does, however, concentrate on the architectural juxtapostion of the grand, decorative dome of the Scottish Provident Building in Donegall Square (the figure atop the dome is no longer in position) and the more mundane gable wall, roofs and chimneys of the surrounding buildings of Fountain Street. The style of the painting is somewhat reminiscent of the work of the artist Rose Barton.

JANUARY 2003

MONDAY 6

THURSDAY 9

TUESDAY 7

FRIDAY 10

WEDNESDAY 8

SATURDAY 11 / SUNDAY 12

JANUARY 2003

MONDAY 13

THURSDAY 16

TUESDAY 14

FRIDAY 17

WEDNESDAY 15

SATURDAY 18 / SUNDAY 19

List of Illustrations

List of Illustrations

Acknowledgements

The publisher wishes to thank the following for permission to reproduce work in copyright:

Basil Blackshaw for *A Road* by Basil Blackshaw; Aodh Bourke for *Summer Evening, Achill* by Michael J. Bourke; Laillí Lamb de Buitléar for *A Connemara Lake* by Charles Lamb; Margaret Campbell for *Red Mill, Whitehouse* by Arthur Campbell; T.P. Flanagan for *Blue Shore* by T.P. Flanagan; Geraldine Hone for *Ruin at Ardmore* by Evie Hone; Rhoda McGuinness for *Village by the Sea* by Norah McGuinness; Cecil Maguire for *Long Walk from Claddagh Quay, Galway* by Cecil Maguire; J. Middleton for *September Evening, Ballymote* by Colin Middleton; Dr Michael Purser as representative of the Heirs and Successors of Mainie Jellett for *Coast Scene (Dooagh, Achill Island)* by Mainie Jellett; Patsy Dan Rodgers for *Tory in a Storm* by Patsy Dan Rodgers; Dorothy B. Stevenson for *Breakers, Achill* by Patric Stevenson; Kenneth Webb for *Farm and Trees* by Kenneth Webb; *The Potato Gatherers* by George Russell is reprinted by permission of Russell & Volkening as agents for the Estate of George Russell.

While every effort has been made to contact copyright holders, the publisher would welcome information on any oversight which may have occurred.

Text by Paul Harron (Editor)

The publisher also wishes to thank Pat McLean, Rights and Reproductions Officer, Ulster Museum; Martyn Anglesea, Keeper of Fine Art, Ulster Museum; and Catherine McCullough, Curator, Armagh County Museum, for all their help in compiling this collection.